# CAN I WILL COOK! COOK!

## Everyday Cooking for Everyday People

R.

# CONTENTS

# Introduction

This book reflects a desire to instil healthier eating habits into all communities. For many years now, a strategy of both Government and the media has been to instruct us all about the benefits of eating healthy foods and how choosing those foods will prolong our health and improve our overall wellbeing.

Clearly, eating well and enjoying yourself whilst doing so will have some of those benefits, but for many people whose lives are busy managing an everyday struggle, due maybe to the pressures of running a family or making ends meet, the practice of eating healthily and enjoying the pleasure of preparing food to sit and enjoy is that much harder.

Can Cook Will Cook acknowledges these difficulties but sets out to show that whatever your circumstances and however busy you are, you can always find something interesting to cook and the time to cook and enjoy the food you have cooked. Furthermore, with a bit of commitment and routine, you will realise that wanting to cook and to share the cooking experience can become a really exciting part of your day – everyday.

We hope you enjoy using the book, preparing these simple recipes, experimenting with food and sharing your cooking experience with your family and friends. There is something in here for everyone.

# About Sure Start and Fresh Cafés

Sure Start is all about giving children and parents the best chance to strongly live and thrive as a family and as individuals. Our Sure Start has been around since 2000 and has done some amazing work with hundreds of families who otherwise would have had little or no support. Every year we look for new ways to work with people and improve the chances of children. This year we decided (amongst everything else that goes on) to 'play' with food and all the great things you can do with it.

To get started we used our cafés as a base we now have 3 cafés trading under the brand "Fresh". Through Fresh, we have started to get a small number of people, either as customers or as our trainees, to think about their diet and view cooking and eating as fun. Then as a consequence of all this activity, we have been going along creating a neat little business.

Now we want to spread our methods to a wider and much larger audience. The creation of this book, which, together with the ideas we have to expand our services, will in the coming years hopefully see us grow into a vibrant and commercially strong social enterprise, creating lots of opportunity and jobs along the way.

For more information visit www.surestartspeke.org

# The Can Cook Initiative

If you can cook, are comfortable cooking and cook regularly and confidently, this book is not really for you – although we bet you find something in here that you will want to try. However, if you think you can't cook (and everybody can) and so won't cook (or rarely feel the urge to) this book is very much for you. It is packed with easy recipes and made up of really tasty foods available from every supermarket.

At our community cafés, we have always experimented by introducing new foods into our menu and tempting our customers away from the bad habits and convenience that make meal times something of a chore rather than being one of the most important parts of the day. For us, we want to encourage people to sit down, relax, taste, discuss their food and then later, to go home and prepare the same types of food for their families.

Can Cook Will Cook was originally a short training course to introduce basic cookery techniques to people who hardly ever cooked and who viewed the need for such things as herbs and spices in cooking as something quite alien, even 'weird'. The training was a great success and it inspired us to want to share some of the recipes we and our trainees have used with you.

Our slogan is "Everyday Cooking for Everyday People" and our passion is about just that – getting everyone to enjoy food, every single day. We have a great time managing our cafés, teaching people the basics of cookery and creating new ways to share this experience with anyone who is starting to cook and / or looking for recipes that are fun and easy to prepare.

This is not a celebrity chef book with lots of researchers and a big budget to make it all incredibly slick. This is a book about us all mucking in to get it done and real grass roots cookery. If we can get you to take time to play with our recipes – and as you become more confident swop and change the ingredients to create versions you can call your own – Can Cook Will Cook will have achieved much of what it set out to do.

Please read it, use it, get it messy and let us know all about it.

robbie.davison@surestartspeke.org

# Tony and the Trainees

3 years ago Tony became our chef. He joined us saying "I want a new challenge, to cook and do something different far away from restaurants". Slowly but surely, and with many successes along the way, he and his café colleagues (Angie, Margie and Di) started to change the way food is served at our centre. With a new type of community café in place, he and the team – ready for another challenge – jumped right into teaching parents how to cook.

The faces you see throughout this book are of Tony, the parents (and sometimes grandparents) and their children who have either taken part in our training or who came along to one of our 'foodie' events.

The pictures tell their own stories...

09

# Things you might need

All the ingredients in our recipes are available from supermarkets.
We hope you are lucky enough to have a specialist deli or good butcher or
fishmonger nearby to enable you to 'keep it local' but in the real world we
know for most people this is not always an option, so supermarkets it is.

That said, you will need a few utensils – we are not saying go out and buy
everything at once, just pick bits up as you need them. We have provided
a guide price for you to purchase items that will do the job.

Two sharp knives, one 8 inch, one 4 inch = £12 for the two
Two plastic chopping boards, one for meat, one for veg = £5
A pestle and mortar to crush up your spices = £5 – £8
A hand blender for your soups= £10 – £20
A measuring jug = £1
A couple of wooden spoons = £2
A colander = £2
A large plastic mixing bowl for all those salads and desserts = £3
Scales = £5
A potato ricer for the smoothest mash ever (Ikea have good ones) = £5
A garlic press, for times when you don't want to chop = £3
Ramekin dishes for starters or serving and baking little puds = 5 for £10

## How much?

 Alongside each recipe we have calculated an approximate
cost to help you budget for each meal. Each price assumes
you have a stock of items such as herbs, spices and oils.

# 5-a-day

Eating five portions of fruit and vegetables every day is the simplest way for your body to get the vitamins, minerals and other nutrients it needs. You can start by including two portions with each of your meals.

## Easy ways to get 5-a-day

Add fruit and veg to your favourite recipes – such as peppers and sweetcorn to pasta sauces and pizza toppings, peas and beans to soups, root veg to mashed potato.

Snack on fresh and dried fruit. Fruit is less fattening than most processed snacks, and a healthy alternative for mid-morning or mid-afternoon.

Have a fruity pudding or add fruit to your breakfast. Don't stop at strawberry yogurts – try adding banana or fresh blueberries to your cereal or raisins to your porridge.

Use frozen veg if it's easier. It counts.

Eat more beans and pulses. Adding them to salads is easy and canned butter or kidney beans are quick to prepare – just make sure they're low in salt.

Make a smoothie for breakfast by blending your favourite fruits together.

## What counts as one of my five a day?

All fruit and vegetables count: fresh, frozen, canned or dried; with the following exceptions:

Pure fruit juices and fruit smoothies only count as one portion per day, no matter how much you drink.
Beans and pulses can only count as one portion per day.
Potatoes don't count at all.

## What's a 5-a-day portion?

As a general rule, a portion is 80g of fruit and veg which is roughly a handful. The following all count as 1 portion:

1 apple, banana, pear, orange
2 plums, satsumas, kiwi fruit
half a grapefruit or avocado
1 large slice of melon or pineapple
3 heaped tablespoons of veg, beans and pulses, or fruit salad
1 heaped tablespoon of raisins or sultanas
3 dried apricots
1 cupful of grapes, cherries or berries
1 dessert bowlful of salad
1 small glass (150ml) of pure fruit juice

## How to get the most nutrition from fruit and veg

Preparing fruit and veg can cause some of the vitamins and minerals to be lost. Here's how to keep hold of them:

Eat fresh fruit and veg as soon as possible.
Don't overcook; crunchy is healthy.
Cook in as little water as possible or steam.
Don't leave cut veg open to air, light or heat.
Don't keep food hot for too long.

# SOUPS

We love soups, everybody loves soups.
They're so quick and easy and last for days.
Try these out to get you started.

# Celeriac and Potato Soup

Fry off the onion and garlic in the butter and olive oil on a low heat until soft, taking care not to colour the garlic (this should take about 5 minutes).

Add the thyme leaves, potatoes, celeriac and stock and bring to the boil, then simmer for about 40 minutes until the vegetables are tender.

Add the cream then bring back to the boil and purée the mixture with a hand blender until smooth and silky. Season according to your taste with salt and pepper.

Pour into 4 soup bowls and garnish with some flat leaf parsley and finely sliced celery.

INGREDIENTS
2 white onions diced
4 cloves of garlic chopped
2 knobs of butter
A splash of olive oil
2 tbls of thyme leaves
400g of celeriac cubed
400g of potatoes cubed
2 pints of vegetable stock
100ml of double cream
Salt and pepper

Serves 4

£3.50

# Leek and Potato Soup

Fry the onion and garlic in the butter and olive oil on a low heat until soft but not coloured (this should take about 5 minutes).

Add the potatoes, leeks and stock, bring to the boil then simmer for about 30 minutes until the vegetables are tender.

Add the cream and mustard then bring back to the boil and purée the mixture with a hand blender until smooth and silky. Season according to your taste.

Pour into soup bowls and garnish with quickly fried shredded leeks.

Serve with warm crusty bread.

INGREDIENTS
2 onions diced
2 cloves of garlic chopped
2 knobs of butter
A splash of olive oil
600g of leeks
1 tbls of Dijon mustard
300g of potatoes cubed
2 ½ pints of vegetable stock
100ml of double cream
Salt and pepper

Serves 4

£4.00

# Rich Roast Tomato and Basil Soup

Pre-heat the oven to gas mark 6. Slice the tomatoes in half and place into an oven proof dish, then peel and slice the onions and garlic and add to the same dish. Sprinkle over the balsamic vinegar, olive oil and sugar, then mix and bake in the oven for about 1 hour, stirring from time to time until they have softened and coloured.

Transfer to a large saucepan, add the stock and simmer over a medium heat for about 25 – 30 minutes or until the vegetables start to disintegrate. Stir in the basil and liquidise.

Finally, pass the soup through a sieve and season according to your taste.

Serve with warm bread.

INGREDIENTS
1.5kg of tomatoes
4 large red onions
4 tbls of balsamic vinegar
2 tsp of caster sugar
4 tbls of olive oil
3 pints of vegetable stock
2 large handfuls of fresh basil
2 cloves of garlic
Salt and pepper

Serves 4

£4.00

# Mushroom and Tarragon Soup

In a large saucepan heat the olive oil and butter, then add the onions and garlic and cook on a low to medium heat for about 10 minutes.

Add the mushrooms, lemon juice and stock and simmer for about 20 – 25 minutes.

Take the pan off the heat and stir through the cream and tarragon, then liquidise until smooth.

Season and serve with warm crusty bread.

INGREDIENTS
400g of button mushrooms
350g of chestnut mushrooms
1 onion sliced
2 cloves of garlic chopped
Juice from $1/2$ a lemon
$1\frac{1}{2}$ pints of vegetable stock
250ml of double cream
4 tbls of chopped fresh tarragon
Salt and pepper
1 tbls of olive oil
50g of butter
Crusty bread (organic is best)

Serves 4

£4.00

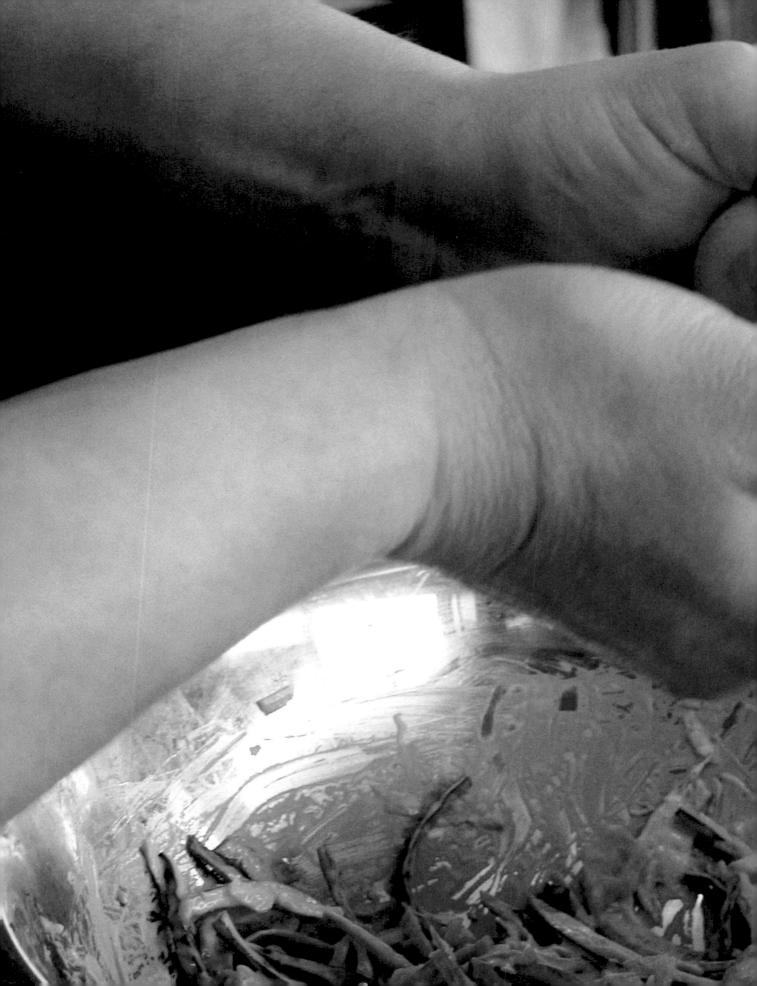

# SALADS

All fresh and full of the taste of summer
with a bit of a twist.

# Tomato and Mozzarella Salad

Slice each tomato into quarters, peel and finely slice the red onion, then place in a bowl.

Tear the basil leaves into the bowl and add the olive oil, ½ a teaspoon of black pepper and 1½ teaspoons of sea salt and mix well.

Take the mozzarella out of its packet and drain off the liquid, then tear it into bite size pieces and stir through the salad. Serve.

Note: When buying the mozzarella you want the type that comes as a soft ball with liquid in a bag or pot, not the hard type used for pizza. Maldon sea salt is a flaky salt with a distinctive taste and works really well with this dish and indeed any other, it is however slightly more expensive. If you don't have Maldon, ordinary salt will do but its not as good.

INGREDIENTS

6 ripe tomatoes
½ a red onion
2 whole mozzarella
10 large fresh basil leaves
3 tbls of olive oil
Maldon sea salt
Black pepper

Serves 4

£3.50

# Rice Salad

Cook the rice according to the instructions on the packet. Once cooked, put the pan into the sink under running cold water to chill, drain well and place the rice into a bowl.

De-seed and dice the peppers and tomatoes, add to the rice. Then peel and dice the onion, chop the celery and add to the rice. De-seed and finely dice the chilli, chop the herbs, then stir into the salad along with the lemon juice and olive oil.

Season according to your taste and serve.

1 cup of long grain rice
1 red pepper
1 green pepper
4 tomatoes
1 red onion
2 sticks of celery
1 red chilli
2 tbls of fresh parsley
2 tbls of fresh mint
2 tbls of olive oil
Juice from 1 lemon
Salt and pepper

**Serves 4**

£3.50

# Roasted Vegetable Salad

Peel and de-seed the butternut squash, slice in half lengthways then slice across the lengths making pieces about 1cm thick and place into an oven proof dish. Next, top and tail the courgette, then slice in half lengthways, and again slice across at about 1cm thick and add to the squash.

De-seed and cube the red pepper and cut the mushrooms into quarters, add both to the pan, then peel and thickly slice the red onion adding to the pan. Next, add the garlic, olive oil and cumin to the vegetables and, using your hands, rub into the vegetables. Add a good pinch of salt and pepper.

Bake the vegetables in a preheated oven at gas mark 6 for 25 – 30 minutes, checking and stirring regularly. The time the vegetables take to cook will vary depending on size but they are ready when they are all quite tender and slightly golden. When they are cooked, remove from the oven, stir through the rocket, and serve immediately with the grated parmesan sprinkled on top.

INGREDIENTS

½ butternut squash
1 courgette
1 red pepper
1 red onion
5 cup mushrooms
1 handful of rocket salad
1 clove of crushed garlic
2 tsp of ground cumin
4 tbls of olive oil
Salt and pepper
3 tbls of grated, fresh parmesan

**Serves 4**

£4.00

# Roasted Vegetable and Couscous

To cook the couscous, place into a bowl and pour enough boiling water over to only just cover, stir well and cover with cling film for 10 minutes.

De-seed and chop the peppers, peel and chop the onion, chop the mushrooms and leek and place all the vegetables into a baking tray along with the thyme and crushed garlic. Sprinkle with olive oil and a little salt and pepper, mix well and bake in a pre-heated oven, gas mark 7 for about 25 minutes, stirring from time to time.

Remove the cling film from the bowl with the couscous and run a fork through it to help it separate. Add the juice from the orange, chop the dill and stir through the couscous.

Finally, add the roasted vegetables and stir well using a tablespoon, season according to your taste and serve hot or cold.

INGREDIENTS

2 cups of couscous
1 red pepper
1 yellow pepper
1 red onion
5 mushrooms
1 leek
1 clove of garlic
3 sprigs of thyme
3 tbls of olive oil
Salt and pepper
3 tbls of fresh dill
Juice from 1 orange

**Serves 4**

£3.50

# Greek Salad

Take off the outer leaves of the lettuce and discard. Wash and dry the inner leaves and place into a bowl.

De-seed and dice the pepper, halve the tomatoes and peel and dice the red onion before adding to the lettuce.

Peel, core and dice the cucumber, slice the olives and add both to the salad.

Mix the olive oil, lemon juice and oregano together and mix into the salad.

Break up the feta cheese and mix carefully into the salad, season with black pepper and serve.

INGREDIENTS

1 little gem lettuce
1 yellow pepper
10 cherry tomatoes
½ a cucumber
½ a red onion
10 pitted black olives
50g of feta cheese
3 tbls of olive oil
Juice from 1 lemon
2 tsp of dried oregano
Black pepper

**Serves 4**

£3.50

# Mixed Bean Salad

Wash and drain the beans and chickpeas and place into a bowl.

Peel and finely dice the red onion, cut the tomatoes into quarters and add to the beans.

Mix the olive oil, balsamic vinegar and finely sliced garlic together and mix into the salad.

Finally, roughly chop the herbs and stir into the salad. Season according to your taste and serve.

INGREDIENTS

200g of red kidney beans
200g of chickpeas
200g of butter beans
200g of borlotti beans
1 red onion
10 cherry tomatoes
½ a clove of garlic
2 tbls of balsamic vinegar
4 tbls of olive oil
2 tbls of fresh dill
2 tbls of fresh coriander
Salt and pepper

**Serves 4**

£3.50

# Salmon Pasta Salad – serves four as a lunch

Bring a large pan of salted water to a rapid boil and cook the pasta according to the instructions on the packet. When cooked, place the pan into the sink under cold running water for about 3 – 5 minutes to cool the pasta down and stop it from cooking any more. Drain and set aside.

While the pasta is cooking cut the salmon into strips and then into about 1cm cubes, place into a bowl along with the olive oil and smoked paprika, mix well and leave for about 10 minutes to marinade.

De-seed and finely slice the peppers, peel and finely slice the red onion and place both into a clean bowl along with the pasta. Heat a frying pan and add all the salmon and olive oil mixture, cook for about 3 minutes on a high heat, then pour all of the salmon and oil into the pasta. Add the lemon zest and juice and the dill, then mix well and season to taste.

INGREDIENTS

300g penne pasta
170g fillet of salmon
1 red pepper
1 yellow pepper
1 red onion
3 tbls of olive oil
1 tsp of smoked paprika
Juice and zest from 1 lemon
2 tbls of chopped fresh dill
Salt and pepper

≠4·00

# Cucumber and Mint Salad

Cut the cucumber in half lengthways and using a teaspoon scrape out the seeds from the middle.

Cut the cucumber at a slight angle in ½ cm thick slices and place into a bowl, then peel and very finely slice the onion, adding it to the cucumber.

Shred the mint leaves and add to the salad along with the yoghurt and lemon juice, stir and let stand for a couple of minutes. Season according to your taste and serve.

INGREDIENTS

1 cucumber
1 white onion
3 tbls of mint leaves
4 tbls of Greek yoghurt
Juice from ½ a lemon
Salt and pepper

₤2.00

# Tuna Pasta Salad – serves four as a lunch

Bring a large pan of salted water to a rapid boil and cook the pasta according to the instructions on the packet. When cooked, place the pan into the sink under cold running water for about 5 minutes to cool the pasta down and stop it from cooking any more. Drain and set aside.

While the pasta is cooking, open the tuna and drain off the brine, squeezing out as much as you can, then place into a bowl along with the drained pasta.

Peel and finely dice the red onion then de-seed and finely dice the peppers adding to the pasta. Add the juice from the lemon and the mayonnaise then mix well. Stir through the tarragon and season according to your taste. Serve with a handful of mixed leaves.

INGREDIENTS

300g penne pasta
2 small cans of tuna
1 red onion
1 green pepper
1 red pepper
Juice from 1 lemon
6 tbls of mayonnaise
2 tbls of chopped fresh tarragon
Salt and pepper
4 good handfuls of mixed leaves

₤2.50

# POTATOES +VEG

No meat or fish, just simple dishes that concentrate on spreading the word about the versatility of potatoes and veg.

# Creamy Garlic Potatoes

Place the potatoes into a pan of cold water and bring to the boil, turn down the heat and simmer for about 20 – 25 minutes until only just cooked. Take off the heat and drain until slightly cooled, then cut the potatoes in half lengthways and place into an oven proof dish.

In a bowl, mix the wine, cream and garlic together, add a good pinch of salt and pepper and pour over all of the potatoes, lightly stir in the thyme and give it a little shake.

Bake the potatoes in a pre-heated oven on gas mark 7 for about 10 – 15 minutes.

INGREDIENTS

600g of new potatoes
300ml of double cream
100ml of white wine
2 cloves of crushed garlic
3 sprigs of thyme
Salt and pepper

Serves 4

£2.20

(if you already have wine in the house)

28

# Herby Potatoes

Place the potatoes in their skins into a pan of cold water and bring to the boil, then turn down the heat and simmer for about 20–25 minutes until only just cooked. When cooked, drain and leave to cool slightly, peel the skin off, then cut in half lengthways.

Heat the olive oil in a pan and start to fry the potatoes, after 2 minutes add the garlic and continue to fry on high heat for a further 5 minutes, stirring and moving the potatoes so they don't stick but become slightly coloured.

Remove the potatoes from the heat and stir through the herbs, let stand for a minute or two and season to taste. Serve immediately.

INGREDIENTS

600g of new potatoes
1 clove of crushed garlic
1 tbls of chopped fresh dill
1 tbls of chopped fresh parsley
½ tbls of chopped fresh mint
3 tbls of olive oil
Salt and pepper

Serves 4

£2.50

# Moroccan Spiced Vegetables

Bring a pan of water to the boil, then peel and slice the carrots about 2cm thick, place into the pan and cook rapidly for 2–3 minutes. Remove the carrots with a slotted spoon and set aside.

In the same pan cook the cauliflower for 2–3 minutes, remove and set aside with the carrots.

Peel and dice the butternut squash then de-seed and dice the pepper and put all of the vegetables into an oven proof dish.

Top and tail the aubergine, slice it lengthways about 2cms thick, then dice into 2cm chunks adding to the rest of the vegetables. Add the olive oil, ground cumin, chilli powder and cinnamon to the vegetables, mix well with your hands, then bake in a pre-heated oven at gas mark 7 for about 20–25 minutes checking and stirring from time to time. Remove and serve with the rice.

INGREDIENTS

2 carrots
½ a butternut squash
1 green pepper
1 aubergine
4 cauliflower florets
4 tbls of olive oil
1 tbls of ground cumin
½ a tsp of chilli powder
1 tsp of ground cinnamon
1 tbls of chopped, fresh coriander
Salt and pepper
3 small cups of organic long grain rice cooked using the instructions on the pack

Serves 4

£4.50

# Potato, Chickpea and Broad Bean Salad

Place the potatoes into a pan of cold water and bring to the boil, then turn down the heat and simmer for about 15 – 20 minutes until only just cooked. When cooked, place the pan into the sink under cold running water to cool them down and stop them cooking any further.

While the potatoes are cooking, open the chickpeas and broad beans and rinse them in a colander under cold running water. When the potatoes are cool, slice them in half lengthways and place into a bowl along with the beans and chickpeas. Now peel and finely slice the red onion, adding to the bowl. Add the juice and the olive oil, and then stir through the coriander, season according to your taste and serve.

INGREDIENTS

400g new potatoes
1 can of chickpeas
1 can of broad beans
1 red onion
4 tbls of olive oil
Juice from 2 oranges
2 tbls of chopped fresh coriander
Salt and pepper

**Serves 4**

23.00

# Stir Fried Vegetables

Bring a large pan of water to a rapid boil, peel and slice the carrots at an angle about 1cm thick and place them into the water. Cook for about 2–3 minutes until slightly tender but still a little crisp. When cooked remove from the pan with a slotted spoon and set aside.

The next step is to remove the florets from the cauliflower and when the water is back to a rapid boil place them in the pan and cook for 2–3 minutes, then remove and set aside. Repeat the process with the broccoli.

When all the vegetables are cooked, peel and slice the onion, heat the oil in a frying pan and fry the onions and garlic. After a couple of minutes, add the rest of the vegetables and stir fry for about 2 minutes on a high heat. Add the spices and continue to stir fry for a further 3 minutes. Season according to your taste and serve.

INGREDIENTS

1 small head of broccoli
1 small head of cauliflower
2 large carrots
1 red onion
1 tsp of cumin seeds
1 tsp of ground cumin
1 tsp of ground coriander
1 clove of crushed garlic
3 tbls of olive oil
Salt and pepper

**Serves 4**

22.50

# Tandoori Potatoes

Place the potatoes into a pan of cold water, bring to the boil, then turn down the heat and simmer for about 15–20 minutes until only just cooked. When cooked take off the heat and drain until slightly cooled, then cut the potatoes in half lengthways and set aside.

In a bowl mix the tandoori paste and the yoghurt, then heat a frying pan with the oil and start to fry the potatoes, when slightly coloured add the tandoori and yoghurt mixture and continue to cook for 1–2 minutes on a high heat, then remove from the heat and stir through the lemon juice and coriander. Finely slice the spring onions and stir through, then season with salt if needed.

INGREDIENTS
600g of new potatoes
3 tbls of tandoori paste
(ready mixed jars are fine)
5 spring onions
2 tbls of natural plain yoghurt
Juice from 1/2 a lemon
2 tbls of fresh, chopped coriander
3 tbls of vegetable oil
Salt

Serves 4

£2.20

# MAIN COURSES

These dishes are all about the 'Can Cook' trainees and the sessions they had with our chef Tony. Here you'll find stews, curries, pasta, noodles – all meaty, fishy, spicy and oozing with flavour.

# ALISON'S STUFFED CHICKEN WITH LINGUINE

JUST FOR YOU

INGREDIENTS
1 chicken breast beaten flat
30g of stilton
Knob of butter
½ a tbls of cream
1 tbls of chopped parsley
2 rashers of bacon
Olive oil
40ml of white wine
40ml of stock
1 tbls of corn flour
5 button mushrooms sliced
Salt and pepper
Linguine

£3.00

Beat and press the chicken breast until flat.

In a bowl mix together the stilton, butter, cream and parsley.
Season and spread all over the chicken breast.

Roll the chicken up and wrap the bacon around it, secure with cocktail sticks,
heat a pan with a little oil and fry the chicken until the bacon is golden all over.

Pour in the wine, stock and mushrooms, then simmer covered for about
30 minutes turning occasionally.

Blend the cornflour in a cup with a little cold water and add to the pan,
stirring until thickened. When cooked remove and keep warm.

Bring a pan of water to the boil and cook the pasta as per instructions on
packet. Serve the chicken on top of the pasta with the sauce poured over
the top.

# AMY'S NORMANDY CASSEROLE
## – SERVES TWO

INGREDIENTS
1 onion peeled and quartered
1 clove of garlic crushed
½ a stick of celery sliced
1 chicken breast diced
150ml of apple juice
200ml of water
1 carrot peeled and sliced
5 button mushrooms quartered
1 apple, peeled, cored and quartered
½ tin of broad beans
½ tbls of soy sauce
Olive oil
1 tbls of flour
Salt and pepper

£3.⁰⁰

Heat 1 tbls of olive oil in a pan and fry the onions, garlic, celery and chicken for about 5 minutes, then sprinkle the flour into the pan, stirring constantly for 4 minutes before gradually adding the apple juice.

Bring to the boil while stirring then turn down the heat to a simmer and add the carrots and soy sauce – put a lid on the pan and gently simmer for about 30 minutes, checking now and again, adding a little water if needed.

After 40 minutes add the mushrooms, apple and broad beans, cover and cook for a further 20 minutes, check seasoning, maybe add a little black pepper and serve.

# ANITA'S CHICKEN AND CHUNKY SWEET POTATO SOUP
## - SERVES TWO

INGREDIENTS
1 sweet potato
1 chicken breast
1 clove of garlic, crushed
1 onion
2 tsp paprika
1/2 a tin of tomatoes
100ml of vegetable stock
1/2 carrot finely diced
1/2 red pepper diced
1 tbls of tomato purée
2 tbls of rice noodles
1 tbls of oregano
1 tbls of basil olive oil
Salt and pepper

₤3.00

Peel and dice the sweet potato to about 1cm thick. Place in a pan of water, bring to the boil and simmer for about 5 minutes. Drain and set aside.

Slice the chicken into thin strips and place into a bowl with 1/2 the crushed garlic, 1 teaspoon of the paprika and a little olive oil and set aside.

To make the base of the soup, dice the onion and crush the remaining garlic and fry gently in a pan for about 5 minutes. Add the carrot and pepper and continue frying for a further 5 minutes. Stir in the tomatoes, vegetable stock and sweet potatoes and bring to the boil then simmer for 10 minutes. Add the rice noodles, oregano, basil, tomato purée and paprika. Season to taste and keep warm.

Finally, heat a little olive oil in a pan and fry the chicken for about 6 minutes until cooked through, season and serve the soup in a bowl with the chicken on top. Garnish with a little more fresh oregano.

# BECKY'S SESAME SALMON NOODLES

### A MEAL FOR ONE

INGREDIENTS
1 small fillet of salmon
1 tbls of sesame seeds
1 large handful of cooked egg noodles
1 red pepper deseeded and sliced
1/2 a red onion peeled and sliced
2 tbls of bean sprouts
2 tbls of chopped coriander
1 tsp of sesame oil
1 tsp of vegetable oil
1 inch piece of grated ginger
1 spring onion finely sliced
1 tbls of sweet chilli sauce
1 tbls of soy sauce

£2.50

Dip the top side of the salmon into the sesame seeds and fry in a hot pan with a little oil for about 4 minutes on each side. Remove and keep warm in a low oven.

Heat a pan with the vegetable oil and sesame oil and stir fry the peppers and onion for about 3 minutes. Add the ginger, bean sprouts, noodles, chilli sauce and soy sauce, continue to fry for a further 2 minutes then quickly stir in the coriander for a few seconds.

Serve, placing the noodles into the centre of a plate and the salmon on top. To finish, sprinkle the spring onions onto the salmon.

# DEBBIE'S RUSTIC LAMB STEW FOR TWO

INGREDIENTS
4 tomatoes chopped
½ an aubergine cubed
1 courgette cubed
1 green pepper chopped
2 onions diced
2 cloves of garlic crushed
400g of cubed lamb
400ml of water
1 tbls of cumin
1 tbls of cinnamon
2 bay leaves
2 potatoes cubed
Salt and pepper

£5.50

Fry the onions and garlic in a little oil and then add the lamb and spices and continue to fry for a few minutes until browned.

Add the water and bay leaf. Cover and simmer for about 35–45 minutes until tender. Add a little more water if it starts to become a bit dry.

Now add all of the other ingredients and continue to cook until the vegetables are tender. Season according to your taste and serve with some green beans.

# IAN'S SALMON WRAPPED IN BACON FOR YOU AND A FRIEND

INGREDIENTS
2 fillets of salmon
4 rashers of smoked bacon
8 new potatoes
1 red pepper
1 red onion
1 courgette
Olive oil
A handful of fresh basil
Salt and pepper

24.50

Slice the salmon lengthways and wrap with the bacon, set aside.

Place the potatoes in a pan of cold water and bring to the boil then simmer for 15 – 20 minutes until just cooked, remove from pan and leave to cool slightly.

Heat a frying pan with a little oil and gently fry the salmon for about 4 minutes on each side, when cooked remove and keep warm. Retain the oil in the pan.

De-seed and slice the pepper, slice the onion and courgette and place into a bowl. Slice the potatoes into quarters and add to the bowl along with 2 tbls of olive oil and salt and pepper, then add to the same pan you cooked the fish in and fry for about 7 – 10 minutes stirring all the time.

Remove from the heat and add a handful of chopped basil leaves, then stir and serve on a plate with the salmon on top.

# GEMMA'S STEAK AND COLCANNON POTATOES

INGREDIENTS
400g rump steak
6 medium potatoes cubed
Half a Savoy cabbage sliced
6 spring onions finely sliced
Knob of butter
Olive oil
2 tbls of crème fraiche
2 tbls of tarragon
Salt and pepper

£5.50

Cook the potatoes in a pan of water until tender (about 20 – 25 mins). While the potatoes are simmering away, cook the cabbage in a pan with the butter for about 5 minutes until slightly soft. When the potatoes are soft mash as fine as you can get them, mix in the cabbage, spring onions, then season and keep warm.

Heat a little oil in a pan and fry the steak until cooked (turning occasionally). When cooked add the crème fraiche and tarragon and season according to your taste.

Arrange the potatoes and cabbage mash to the centre of your serving plates and place the steak with the sauce onto the mash.

# GEORGINA'S SPAGHETTI BOLOGNESE FOR TWO

INGREDIENTS
300g of mince
2 onions chopped
2 carrot diced
8 mushrooms sliced
1 glass of red wine
400g tin of tomatoes
2 tsp vegetable stock (or one cube)
Olive oil
Salt and pepper
4 tbls of chopped basil
Pasta cooked according to instructions
on the pack.

£4.50

(if you already have wine in the house)

Fry the mince and onions in a pan until the mince is browned (a couple of minutes), then add the red wine and reduce until the wine has nearly disappeared.

Add the tomatoes, carrot, mushrooms and stock and simmer for about 30 minutes stirring every now and again, adding a little water if needed. When cooked add the basil and season to taste, serve on top of the pasta.

Buy the best quality dried pasta you can find, it does make a difference.

# JOANNA'S CORNED BEEF HASH WITH SPICED RED CABBAGE

### FOR TWO PEOPLE

INGREDIENTS

For the Red Cabbage:
½ a red cabbage shredded
1 red onion sliced
1 cooking apple, peeled and sliced
½ a tsp of nutmeg
A pinch of ground cinnamon
A pinch of ground cloves
1 tbls of soft brown sugar
2 tbls of white wine vinegar
Knob of butter
1 big tbls of redcurrant jelly

For the Hash:
2 large potatoes, peeled and diced
2 small onions diced
A splash of Worcester sauce
½ a leek washed and sliced
½ a carrot peeled and sliced
200g of corned beef, chopped

£4.00

For the corned beef hash:

Place the carrot and potato into a large pan, cover with water and boil, stirring occasionally until they are cooked and soft. Drain and lightly crush.

Add the onion and leek to a frying pan with a little oil and fry for 5 minutes. Add them to the carrot and potato cooked earlier, together with the corned beef. Sprinkle in the Worcester sauce and season according to your taste.

Flour your hands and mould the mix into two large patties. Fry, turning once, over a medium heat for about 7 – 10 minutes. Serve with the red cabbage.

This is also great with a dollop of red sauce – great comfort food

For the spiced red cabbage:

Place all the ingredients (except the redcurrant jelly) into a large pan and bring to the boil. Cover and simmer for about 1 hour or until the cabbage is tender. Season well with salt and pepper and stir through the red currant jelly. Leave to stand for a couple of minutes and serve. Also works a treat with Pearl's Scouse dish (see page 75).

# LISA'S CHILLI BEEF NOODLES FOR TWO

INGREDIENTS
200g of rump steak
200g of cooked egg noodles
2 tsp of grated ginger
1 clove of crushed garlic
2 tsp of sesame seeds
2 tsp of sesame oil
2 tbls of vegetable oil
½ a red pepper
½ a red onion
4 tbls of bean sprouts
2 tbls of soy sauce
2 tbls of sweet chilli sauce
1 tsp of Chinese 5 spice

£3.20

Slice the steak, onion and pepper into thin strips. Heat a frying pan until very hot then add both oils and stir fry the steak for about 1 minute before adding the pepper and onion. Continue to fry for 2 minutes.

Add the ginger, garlic, soy sauce, sweet chilli sauce, 5 spice and bean sprouts. Cook for 2 minutes then add the noodles and sesame seeds and cook for a further 2 minutes and serve.

Take care when frying with a really hot pan – the oil can spit and burn.

# LORRAINE'S CHILLI CON CARNE FOR TWO

INGREDIENTS
250g of mince
2 onions chopped
1 clove of garlic
1 tbls of olive oil
2 tsp of chilli powder
1 tsp of ground cumin
8 sun dried tomatoes chopped
1 glass of red wine
1 tsp of cinnamon
1 can of kidney beans drained
1 tin of tomatoes
Salt and pepper
Long grain rice

£3.50

(if you already have red wine in the house)

Fry the onions and mince in a pan until the mince is browned. Add the wine and cook until nearly all the wine has been absorbed.

Add the spices and garlic and cook for 2 minutes before adding all of the remaining ingredients except the kidney beans. Cook for 35 minutes stirring now and again adding a little water if needed.

After 20 minutes add the kidney beans and cook for a further 15 minutes. Season according to your taste and serve with rice and / or tortilla chips.

# LYNDSEY'S SALMON WITH DILL AND SPRING ONION MASH FOR TWO

INGREDIENTS
2 fillets of salmon
Zest and juice from 1 lemon
1 tbls of chopped dill
Salt and pepper
4 medium potatoes peeled and chopped
Knob of butter
6 tbls of cream
8 spring onions finely sliced
2 tbls of chopped chives

£4.50

Place the salmon into a bowl along with the dill, zest and juice from the lemon and season.

Put the potatoes into a pan of cold water and bring to the boil, then simmer for about 20 – 25 minutes until cooked. Remove from pan and mash as fine and smooth as you can. Put the mashed potato back into the pan, add the cream and butter and mix well. Season to taste and keep warm.

Heat a little oil in a pan and fry the salmon for about 4 minutes on each side. Remove and keep warm. Stir the spring onions and chives into the mash and serve onto the centre of your serving plate with the salmon on top.

# THE CAN COOK WILL COOK BARBEQUE

Weather permitting (and we got lucky), a barbie provides the ideal place for simple, fresh food that's ready to go in minutes and can be set up almost anywhere you have a bit of outside space – we borrowed a bit of a local park to celebrate the end of our training with our trainees.

Look at the weather forecast, pick a day, take a bit of time to prepare our recipes and let the food take centre stage.

## BBQ BEEFBURGERS

Finely chop or grate the onion and crush the garlic. Heat a little oil in a pan and gently fry the onion and garlic for about 5 minutes until soft but not too coloured, leave to cool.

In a bowl start to squeeze the mince with your hands until it becomes soft and well mixed, then add the paprika, mixed herbs, tomato purée and salt and pepper and combine well.

When the onion mixture has cooled add to the mince and squeeze and scrunch again until everything is well combined. Now shape the mixture into a burger shape and place onto an oiled plate and refrigerate for about 10 minutes.

Heat a little oil in a frying pan and fry the burger for about 4 minutes on each side until cooked and serve in the burger bun along with the lettuce, tomato, cheese and sauce if using.

Makes 10 burgers.

INGREDIENTS
670g minced beef
4 white onions
4 cloves of garlic
1/4 tsp paprika
8 tsp mixed herbs
8 tsp tomato purée
3 tsp salt
4 tsp pepper
10 burger buns
10 slices of cheese
20 slices of tomato
Lettuce

## BBQ CHICKEN KEBABS

In a bowl mix all of the ingredients together, cover and refrigerate for at least 2 hours or preferably overnight.

When the chicken has marinated skewer the chicken and onion onto the wooden skewers – there should be enough for 4 skewers.

Cook them on the barbie for about 10 – 20 minutes depending on how thick you sliced the chicken and how hot the barbie is.

INGREDIENTS
2 chicken breasts sliced lengthways
2 tsp of ground cumin
1 clove of garlic crushed
Juice from 1 lemon
1 tbls of honey
1 tbls of soy sauce
2 tbls of chopped coriander
1 red onion peeled and cut into 8
4 wooden skewers
1 tsp black pepper

## BBQ WHOLE SEA BASS

Lay out the foil on a table and place half the sliced lemons in a line along the middle then lay the fish on top.

Using a sharp knife make a few slices into the fish on both sides, then rub the fennel, olive oil, salt and pepper and lemon juice into the cuts.

Place the dill into the cavity, now bring all four sides of the foil upwards and scrunch together to make something that looks like a bag. Place the fish onto the hottest part of the barbie and cook for 15 – 20 minutes in the foil.

INGREDIENTS
1 whole sea bass gutted and scaled
1 lemon sliced plus the juice from 1 more
A few sprigs of fresh dill
1 tsp of crushed fennel seeds
Pinch of salt and black pepper
2 tbls of olive oil
Enough silver foil to wrap the fish in

# MARCELLA'S SWEET AND TANGY CHICKEN
## FOR TWO HUNGRY PEOPLE OR A LIGHT LUNCH FOR FOUR

INGREDIENTS
2 chicken breasts cut into strips
1 onion diced
1 red pepper sliced
100ml of water
400g tin of chopped tomatoes
½ a can of pineapple cubes and
the juice from the can
1 clove of garlic
1 carrot finely sliced
2 tbls of sweet chilli sauce
2 tsp of tomato purée
2 tbls of olive oil
Cooked rice to serve

£4.00

Heat a pan with the olive oil and fry the chicken and onion for about 5 minutes before adding the garlic, pepper, carrot, chilli sauce, tomatoes and pineapple juice. Cook for a further 5 minutes.

Now add the tomato purée and pineapple cubes and cook for a further 2 minutes. Season according to your taste and serve with rice.

# MARIA'S CHICKEN CURRY FOR TWO

INGREDIENTS
4 tomatoes
1 medium onion
3 tbls of vegetable oil
2 tsp of grated root ginger
2 small clove of garlic crushed
2 green chillis
1 tsp of chilli powder
1 tsp of ground coriander
1 tsp of ground cumin
1 tsp of ground turmeric
1 chicken breast
2 large handfuls of spinach
½ a can of green lentils
200ml of coconut milk
Salt and pepper

£3.50

Peel and dice the onion and fry over a low heat for 7 – 10 minutes until soft, coloured but not burnt.

De-seed the tomatoes and chilli, and chop them both. Put the oil into the frying pan, add all the dry spices and the onions and fry for 2 minutes stirring continuously. Next, add the chilli, tomatoes, ginger and garlic, and fry for a further minute. At this point add a touch of salt.

Now add the chicken and fry for 1 minute, tossing the chicken as it cooks. Pour in the coconut milk, stir and bring to the boil. Simmer gently for about 20 minutes.

After 20 minutes add the drained and washed lentils and spinach, and cook for a further 5 minutes. Season according to your taste. Serve with warm naan bread and pilau rice.

# MARY'S KEDGEREE - A NICE LUNCH FOR TWO

INGREDIENTS
75g of brown basmati rice
35g of puy lentils
Pinch of turmeric
½ an onion finely chopped
½ a tsp of ground cumin
½ a tsp of ground coriander
1½ tbls of olive oil
250g of smoked haddock sliced thickly
2 eggs
3 tbls of fresh, coriander chopped

£4.50

SPECIAL EQUIPMENT
You will need a fairly big frying pan for this dish

Place the rice and lentils in a saucepan and add about 250ml of boiling water. Add the turmeric and give the rice and lentils a good stir. Cover with a lid and bring to the boil, then gently simmer for about 20–25 minutes until the rice is just cooked and the lentils are soft. Remove from the heat and leave with the lid on to steam for another 10 minutes or so. If there is still water in the pan cook gently until it has evaporated.

On a low to medium heat, fry the onion, cumin and ground coriander in the oil for about 10 minutes, until soft and translucent. Increase the heat to high and add the haddock and cook for a few minutes. When the haddock is just cooked push to one side of the pan and crack the eggs into the pan. Cook until the whites start to turn solid and break the yolks so they cook quicker (like a scrambled egg). When the eggs are just cooked, briefly stir into the haddock mixture trying to leave some big pieces of egg if you can.

Add the rice mixture to the pan with half the chopped coriander and stir just enough to mix together and warm the rice. Season to taste and serve with the remaining coriander on top.

# MICK'S LAMB CURRY FOR TWO HUNGRY PEOPLE AFTER A GOOD NIGHT OUT

INGREDIENTS
400g of diced lamb
4 tbls of vegetable oil
2 tsp of grated ginger
2 cloves of crushed garlic
1 tsp of turmeric
3 tsp of garam masala
2 tsp of ground coriander
2 tsp of ground cumin
2 tbls of plain yoghurt
2 tsp of chilli powder
2 onions finely chopped
1 can of chopped tomatoes
200ml of water
4 tbls of chopped, fresh coriander
Salt and pepper
3 small cups of basmati rice cooked following
instructions on the pack
Naan bread

£4.50

Fry the onion in the oil for about 5 minutes on a medium heat, then add the ginger and garlic and fry for a further minute before adding all the dry spices and the lamb. Continue frying for another 3 minutes adding a little salt.

Now stir in the tinned tomatoes, add some water, cover the pan and simmer, stirring from time to time, adding more water if needed. After 45 minutes, add the yoghurt and fresh coriander and cook for 2 minutes. Season according to your taste, serve with basmati rice and of course a naan.

# NICKIE'S WARM DUCK SALAD FOR TWO
## (AS A STARTER)

INGREDIENTS
1 duck breast
1 tbls of soy sauce
1 tsp of Chinese five spice
Juice from 1/2 an orange
A dash of sesame oil
1 tbls of vegetable oil
1/2 a yellow pepper
4 cherry tomatoes
1 carrot
2 tbls of bean sprouts
A handful of mixed salad leaves

£4.00

Peel the skin off the duck breast and place the duck into a bowl along with the soy, 5 spice, sesame oil and orange juice. Leave to marinate for about 20 minutes.

Heat a little oil in a frying pan and add the duck to the pan when warm (not too hot or the marinade will burn). Gently fry for about 4 minutes on each side, remove and keep warm.

De-seed and finely slice the yellow pepper, slice the tomatoes into quarters and add to a bowl along with the salad leaves. Peel the carrot and then using the peeler shave the flesh of the carrot into the bowl and add the bean sprouts.

Serve the salad on a plate, slice the duck and place on top then drizzle the juice over the top.

# NICOLA'S LAMB STEW WITH WHITE CABBAGE FOR TWO

INGREDIENTS
400g of cubed lamb (shoulder)
2 knobs of butter
2 tsp of salt
1 tsp of black pepper
1 tsp of ground cinnamon
2 tsp of ground cumin
2 tsp of paprika
2 onions sliced
¼ white cabbage sliced
2 carrots sliced
2 tbls of sugar
500ml of water

Heat a pan, add the butter and fry the onion and lamb. As the lamb changes colour add the spices and cook for a minute or so. Sprinkle on the sugar and then add all the other ingredients.

Bring the stew to the boil, cover and simmer for about 50 – 60 minutes, stirring from time to time and adding a little water if needed.

Season to taste and serve with a hearty portion of spring onion mash.
(See page 56 for recipe)

# PEARL'S REAL LIVERPUDLIAN SCOUSE FOR A FAMILY OF FOUR

INGREDIENTS
4 tbls of vegetable oil
600g of chuck steak
1 onion chopped
2 carrots peeled and chopped
3 small leeks sliced
2 large potatoes diced
1ltr of beef stock
6 tbls of flour
Salt and pepper
3 tsp of Worcester sauce

£4.50

Cut the steak into chunks, season with salt, coat in the flour and pat off any excess.

Heat a large pan with a little oil and fry the steak until browned. Stir continually to prevent the steak from sticking to the pan. Add the stock and the rest of the vegetables, cover and simmer for about 1 hour or until meat is tender. Keep checking and add more water if it starts to dry towards the end of the hour.

Season according to your taste. We like it with lots of black pepper, particularly on cold nights. Serve with warm buttered bread. This really works with spiced red cabbage. (See page 51 for recipe).

# REBECCA'S SINGAPORE FRIED NOODLES FOR TWO

INGREDIENTS
30g of cashew nuts
½ a tsp of coriander seeds
½ a tsp of cumin seeds
½ a tsp of chilli powder
4 tbls of groundnut oil
250ml of coconut milk
140g of rice noodles
1 chicken breast
2 small red chillis
4 spring onions
2 tomatoes
100g of tofu
Salt and pepper
A large handful of fresh coriander

£3.50

NOTES
You will need a large frying pan or wok for this dish.
Use ready cooked noodles to make things easier.

Put the cashew nuts, coriander seeds, cumin seeds and chilli powder into a pestle and mortar and pound until everything is ground up. Heat half the oil in a frying pan and fry the spice mixture for 1 minute. Slowly stir in the coconut milk, bring to the boil and simmer for 5 minutes then set aside.

As the coconut milk simmers, place the rice noodles into a bowl, cover with boiling water and leave to stand for 2 – 3 minutes. Drain the noodles and leave to stand.

Cut the chicken into strips. Core, de-seed and chop the chilli. Slice the spring onions and roughly chop the tomato. Drain the tofu and cut into 3cm cubes. Heat the remaining oil in a frying pan and stir fry the chicken for 3 minutes or until browned. Add the chilli and spring onions and stir fry for a further 2 minutes.

Add the roughly chopped tomato, diced tofu, the rice noodles and coconut mixture to the pan and stir fry for another 2 minutes or until the whole thing is heated through. Season to your taste with salt and pepper. Roughly chop the fresh coriander, sprinkle over the top and serve.

# STACEY'S SALMON WITH ROCKET AND CRUSHED POTATOES
## - A QUICK MEAL FOR YOU

INGREDIENTS
200g of salmon fillet
200g of new potatoes
3 spring onions
1 tbls of fresh chopped dill
A small handful of rocket leaves
1 tsp smoked paprika
Juice from ½ a lemon
3 tbls of olive oil
Salt and pepper

£2.50

Place the potatoes into a pan of cold water and bring to the boil then simmer with the lid on for about 15 – 20 minutes until just tender.

While the potatoes are cooking, slice the salmon in half, length ways, place into a bowl along with the paprika, lemon juice, 1 tbls of olive oil and a pinch of salt and pepper. Gently rub it all into the fish and set aside.

When the potatoes are cooked, drain and crush with a fork, then finely slice the spring onions and add to the potatoes along with the dill, rocket and the remaining olive oil. Season and mix well, then keep warm.

Heat a pan with a little olive oil and cook the salmon for about 1 – 2 minutes on each side, then serve the potatoes on a plate with the salmon on top.

# SAMANTHA'S BALSAMIC CHICKEN AND HERBY POTATOES FOR TWO

INGREDIENTS
2 chicken breasts
2 tbls of balsamic vinegar
2 tbls of honey
2 tbls of wholegrain mustard
2 cloves of garlic crushed
400g of new potatoes
2 tbls of chopped tarragon
2 tbls of chopped parsley
Salt and pepper
2 handfuls of watercress
1 lemon

£5.00

Slice each chicken breast into 3 pieces and put into a bowl along with the balsamic vinegar, honey, mustard and garlic. Mix well, then set aside.

Place the potatoes into a pan with enough cold water to cover them, bring to the boil and simmer for about 15 – 20 minutes or until tender. Drain and allow them to cool slightly. When cool enough to handle, peel the skins off and slice in half then set aside.

Heat a frying pan with a little oil, take the chicken breast out of the marinade and fry for about 5 minutes on each side until cooked. Take off the heat, season with salt and pepper and leave in the pan to keep warm.

Heat another frying pan with 2 tablespoons of olive oil and fry the potatoes for about 5 minutes until slightly coloured and heated through. Add the chopped tarragon and parsley and the juice from half the lemon. Season to your taste.

Squeeze the juice from the other half of the lemon over the watercress and serve all three together.

# TONY'S NANS MEATBALLS

### – SERVES FOUR FOR LUNCH

INGREDIENTS
500g of lean minced beef
2 onions
2 cloves of garlic crushed
1 tbls of dry basil
2 tbls of chopped fresh oregano
2 tbls of chopped fresh basil
2 tins of chopped plum tomatoes
Olive oil
1 tsp of sugar
Salt and pepper
Egg pasta cooked following the
instructions on the pack

£4.50

Peel and very finely dice the onions. Heat a frying pan with a little olive oil and gently fry one of the onions until soft for about 5 minutes then set aside.

In a large pan, heat a little olive oil and fry the other onion and 1 clove of garlic until they start to colour, then add the chopped tomatoes, sugar and dry basil. Bring to a gentle simmer and leave for about 20 minutes stirring from time to time. Add a little water if needed.

In a large bowl, mix the mince, the onion we cooked first, 1 chopped clove of garlic, the fresh herbs, 1 tsp of salt and ½ tsp pepper. Squash everything together with your hands until it's all combined well. Mould the mixture into balls by rolling it in your hands. They should be a little bigger than golf balls.

Heat a frying pan with a little olive oil and fry the meatballs just enough to colour, then add them to the tomato sauce, cover and simmer for 20 – 25 minutes. Season the tomato sauce to your taste and serve on a nice bed of pasta. You could add a little parmesan cheese to this.

# DESSERTS

Everyone has a childhood favourite.
Here are some of ours.

# Bakewell Tart

## Making the pastry

Roll out the pastry and press into a 4 inch loose bottom flan dish or until it's about as thick as a pound coin throughout. Prick the pastry base with a fork and chill for 20 minutes in the fridge.

Line the pastry with greaseproof paper, pour the rice onto the paper then bake in the oven on gas mark 4 for about 20 minutes (the weight of the rice stops the pastry puffing up). After 20 minutes, remove from the oven, remove the greaseproof paper and rice and let it cool down.

## Making the frangipane mix

Combine the butter and sugar in a bowl until smooth. Add the ground almonds and blend together. Add the cornflour and flour, then add the egg and egg white and mix until very smooth. Add in the vanilla and almond extract to bind.

## To finish off...

Spread a little jam over the bottom of the pastry case, add the frangipane mix on top and bake in the oven for about 30 minutes until the frangipane is puffed, golden brown and firm to the touch.

INGREDIENTS
80g of soft butter
130g of caster sugar
½ a cup of ground almonds
1 tsp of cornflour
2 tsp of flour
1 egg
1 egg white
1 tsp of vanilla extract
2 tsp of almond extract
Raspberry jam
1 pack of shortcrust pastry

ADDITIONAL EQUIPMENT
A loose based flan dish
Greasproof paper
A cup of rice to use as a weight

£3.00

# STICKY TOFFEE PUDDING DAY

Sticky toffee pudding has always been a firm favorite in our cafés. We had lots of requests to put the recipe into the book. So we thought, lets make a day of it (well an afternoon really) and get a few mums and their children in to all have a go and make some puds.

**The Cast**
**Jenny and Ellie** – Jenny is a midwife at our centre.
**Angie, Cindy, Toni and David** – Angie works in our cafés and had hardly cooked before joining us.
**Liz, Will and Lilly** – Liz is the understanding wife of Tony our chef (you see, chefs work long hours)

If you can find a bit of space, try your own sticky toffee session – the kids love it.

## For the pudding

Place the dates into a pan and add the water, put onto a medium heat until the dates have softened. Remove from the heat and blend until smooth. Set the dates aside.

In a large bowl mix together the butter and sugar until light and fluffy using a wooden spoon or an electric whisk if you have one, then add the eggs one by one mixing all the time. Add the flour, baking powder, bicarbonate of soda, golden syrup and puréed dates and combine well.

Grease and flour 4 moulds, divide the mixture between them and bake in a preheated oven gas mark 6 for 20 – 25 minutes until firm to the touch.

## For the sauce

Melt the butter in a pan and stir in the sugar and syrup, then add the double cream and bring to the boil, whisk well and remove from the heat ready to use.

INGREDIENTS

For the pudding:
180g of soft dark brown sugar
60g of soft butter
2 eggs
200g of flour
200g of dried pitted dates
3 tbls of golden syrup
300ml of boiling water
1 tsp of baking powder
1 tsp of bicarbonate of soda

For the sauce:
150ml of double cream
60g of butter
60g of soft dark brown sugar
2 tbls of golden syrup

£3.00

(makes about 6 puddings)

ADDITIONAL EQUIPMENT

Food processor or hand blender to make the date purée.
Electric whisk (optional)

# Simple Rice Pudding

Put all the ingredients into a pan and bring to a gentle simmer.
Cover with a lid and leave to simmer until the milk has been absorbed
and the rice is cooked. It's that easy.

INGREDIENTS
25g of butter
60g of caster sugar
1 pint of milk
1 tsp of vanilla extract
70g of pudding rice

**Serves 4**

# Chocolate Orange Mousse

Break the chocolate into small pieces and place in a bowl over a pan of simmering water, let the chocolate melt slowly. While the chocolate is melting, whip the cream until it forms soft peaks and set aside.

Once the chocolate has melted, remove from the heat and let it cool slightly, then beat in the egg yolks. Once the egg yolks are mixed in fold in the double cream, and then whisk the egg whites to form stiff peaks, fold the orange zest, pour into small glasses and chill for at least 2 hours in your fridge.

How to separate an egg.
Break the egg into the palm of your hand and let the egg white fall through your fingers into a bowl – messy we know, but its fun and it works.

INGREDIENTS
130g of dark chocolate
130ml of double cream
2 eggs (separated, yolks and whites)
2 tsp of orange zest

Serves 2 – 4

£2.50

# SANDWICHES

The staple solution for almost everyone who's in a hurry.
Slow down and try these with friends, family or just as you
ponder your day.

## Steak and Caramelised Onion Baguette

Peel and slice the onion and place in a pan along with the sugar and vinegar and cook on a really low heat for about 1 hour, stirring from time to time. You want the onions to be soft and very sticky but not burnt.

Heat a pan with a little oil and fry the steak to your liking. Set aside once cooked. Slice the baguette in half lengthways and lightly toast. Mix the mayonnaise with both mustards and spread over the baguette.

Take the steak and slice at an angle into bite size pieces. Arrange the steak on the baguettes and cover with the onions. Season according to your taste.

INGREDIENTS
3 white onions
6 tbls of white wine vinegar
3 tbls of soft dark brown sugar
4 baguettes
4 x 100g of rump steak
Salt and pepper
4 tbls of mayonnaise
2 tsp of wholegrain mustard
2 tsp of Dijon mustard

£7.00

## Mature Cheddar and Roast Tomato Baguette for one

Slice the tomatoes in half and lay in an oven proof dish, then divide the basil between the four halves, sprinkle with a pinch of salt and pepper and drizzle with a little olive oil. Cook in a pre-heated oven at gas mark 2 for about 1 hour. Slice the baguette in half lengthways and lightly toast, then spread a little butter and place the cheese onto one side and the tomatoes on top, then put the lid on and serve.

This baguette is always best when serving guests as you can oven roast more tomatoes, otherwise it can be a bit costly just roasting a couple of tomatoes. Alternatively you could roast a load of tomatoes, keep them cool in the fridge and add them to cooked breakfasts or salads through the week.

INGREDIENTS
1 baguette
2 tomatoes
50g of grated mature cheddar
1 tsp of dried basil
Olive oil
Maldon sea salt
Black pepper
Butter

£1.50

## Salmon Wrap with Tartare Sauce for two of you

To make the tartare sauce:
In a bowl mix together the mayonnaise, capers, gherkins, egg, dill and lemon juice then season to your taste.

Slice the salmon in half lengthways and lightly season with salt and pepper. Heat a little oil in a pan and fry the salmon for 1–2 minutes on each side, remove and keep warm in a low oven.

Spread the tartare sauce over the wrap and add the salmon, lettuce, cucumber and spring onions across the middle, then roll the wrap up to form a tube. Slice the wrap in the middle at an angle and serve.

INGREDIENTS
225g fillet of salmon
2 large tortilla wraps
8 thin slices of cucumber
2 small handfuls of shredded iceberg lettuce
4 spring onions sliced
3 tbls of mayonnaise
4 tsp of washed capers
4 tsp of chopped gherkins
Half a boiled egg chopped
1 tbls of chopped fresh dill
2 tsp of lemon juice
Salt and pepper
Olive oil

£2.95

# PASTES, SAUCES + DRESSINGS

For a quick solution there are some great off the shelf versions but if you want to spend a bit of time preparing your own we like these and they work.

# Classic salad dressing

Place the lemon juice and olive oil into a bowl and season with salt and pepper, then add the garlic and allow to infuse for 30 minutes, then remove. Now add the mustard and sugar and stir well. This will go well with salads accompanying chicken or seafood.

INGREDIENTS
2 tbls of olive oil
6 tbls of lemon juice
1 clove of garlic bruised
1 tsp of Dijon mustard
1 tsp of castor sugar
Pinch of salt
2 twists of a black pepper mill

# Indian curry paste

Place all of the ingredients into a food processor and blitz into a paste. This can be used straight away or stored in a jar in the fridge for up to 3 weeks.

INGREDIENTS
2 tsp of garam masala
1 small onion peeled and chopped
2 cloves of garlic chopped
3 inch piece of root ginger peeled and chopped
3 green chillies chopped
1 tsp coriander seeds crushed
2 tomatoes deseeded and chopped
1 tsp of salt
2 tbls of groundnut oil

# Thai curry paste

Place all of the ingredients into a food processor and blitz into a paste. You can use this straight away or it will keep in a sealed jar for about 3 weeks.

INGREDIENTS
5 medium green chillies deseeded
1 onion peeled and chopped
6 inch piece of root ginger peeled and chopped
2 cloves of garlic
1 small bunch of fresh coriander, stalks and all
2 lemongrass stalks chopped
Zest and juice from 1 lime
6 kaffir lime leaves (if you can't get these then replace with the zest from 1 more lime)
1 tbls of coriander seeds crushed
1 tsp of ground cumin
1 tsp of black peppercorns crushed
2 tsp of fish sauce
3 tbls of groundnut oil

# Yoghurt and Cumin dressing

In a bowl mix the yogurt and lemon juice, then add the garlic and mix well to incorporate the garlic then stir through the coriander and season with salt and pepper. This dressing would go well with salads which feature meat dishes especially lamb.

INGREDIENTS
4 tbls of Greek yogurt
1 tbls of lemon juice
1/2 a clove of garlic crushed
2 tsp of ground cumin
1 tbls of chopped coriander
Pinch of salt
Pinch of black pepper

# Kids Lunch boxes

The best place to start your own little '5-a-day' campaign with your children. We think it's all about encouraging healthier habits very early on in their lives. At home around the dinner table is the most important space, but when they trot off to school, the lunch box is the next best place to be. Typically, add some thinly sliced veggies and fruit to a healthy, full fruit drink, a small yogurt and, together with a meat or cheese and tomato cob, there you have it – a full colour healthy food experience, full of vitamins and not a spoon in sight.

As a suggestion try:

Handful of thinly sliced mixed peppers
I carrot again thinly sliced
2 inch piece of cucumber sliced just like the carrot
Slice and core half an apple into bite sized bits
Little bunch of grapes (we have found the kids like red best)
The cob – with your choice of sliced meat or maybe cheese and tomato
Yogurt pouch
Pomegreat drink

Tip: You can now buy lunch boxes for about £6 which have small removable ice packs in – if you can find one, these are the best because everything stays chilled throughout the day.

# Fun facts and figures

During the making of this book 3 trainees gave birth. We trained 22 people – mothers, mothers to be, fathers, fathers to be, grandmothers and one granddad. We used 10 camping stoves, 10 preparation tables, some very sharp knives, brightly coloured chopping boards, pots, pans, bowls, all the necessary shiny utensils and some trendy aprons then we prepared all this food – 12 red cabbages, over 100 red onions, about 20 bunches of spring onions, 50 big carrots, sticks and sticks of celery, 40 kilos of Maris Piper potatoes, 5 kilos of baby potatoes, 70 leeks, 30 cucumbers, 2 very big boxes of tomatoes, 10 tubs of cherry tomatoes, bags of mixed peppers, 5 kilos of mushrooms, 12 courgettes, 50 chicken breasts, a couple of duck breasts, 5 kilos each of beef steak and beef mince, 8 kilos of lamb shoulder, 7 sides of salmon, a large sea bass for the barbie, 50 sardines, 10 bunches of fresh mint, 12 bunches of fresh coriander, 7 bunches of fresh dill, 10 bunches of fresh parsley, 5 bunches each of fresh basil and tarragon (which we grew ourselves), 3 bunches of thyme, 15 bulging bulbs of garlic, 40 lemons, various cheeses, 20 tins of chickpeas, 15 tins of kidney beans, 12 tins of borlotti beans, bags and bags of egg noodles, pasta of varying shapes and sizes, kilos of organic rice, good quality veg and chicken stock, approximately 8 litres of olive oil, a few litres of veg oil, a bottle or two of balsamic vinegar, bottles of red and white wine, 2 bottles of Worcester sauce, 3 bottles of soy sauce, 3 litres of cream, tubs of yogurt, 5 tins of coconut milk, a large catering box of eggs, 20 kilos of plain flour, 4 bottles of white wine vinegar, lots of salt, pepper, nutmeg, cinnamon, garam masala, ground cloves, chilli powder, paprika, cumin, turmeric, coriander powder, mustard, honey and all those other bits that add bite.

ROBBIE

TONY

MIKE

ALEX

## Credits

Can Cook Will Cook concept: **Robbie Davison** (robbie.davison@surestartspeke.org)
Chef: **Tony Evans** (tony.evans@surestartspeke.org)
Design: **Mike Carney / Mike's Studio** (www.mikesstudio.co.uk)
Photography: **Alexandra Wolkowicz** (www.wolkowicz.com)
Additional photography: Mike and Robbie.

## Supporters

**Susan Roberts**, Director, Sure Start Speke (susan.roberts@surestartspeke.org)
**Mark Ord**, Director, Speke Training and Education Centre (mark@stecltd.mersinet.co.uk)
**Julie Curren**, Food and Health Co-ordinator, Liverpool Primary Care Trust (julie.curren@liverpoolpct.nhs.uk)
**Irene Mills**, Public Health Neighbourhood Manager (irene.mills@liverpoolpct.nhs.uk)
**Fiona Shaw**, Director, Capsica (www.loveliverpoolbooks.com)
**Jo Norton**, Community Engagement Officer, (nortonj175@yahoo.co.uk)

Copyright © Sure Start Speke
Photography © Alexandra Wolkowicz

First published in September 2007
Published by Pepper Books, an imprint of Capsica
83 Ampthill Road, Liverpool L17 9QN

Sure Start Speke, Children's Centre,
Conleach Road, Speke, Liverpool L24 0TW
www.surestartspeke.org

A CIP Catalogue record for this book is available from the British Library
ISBN 978-0-955654725

**All proceeds from this book go towards developing services for children and families.**

# People we like

## The Green Fish Café

Dave and his staff run the best café in Liverpool City Centre.

The Green Fish (great name) opened in 1994 and provides really affordable healthy food. The Green Fish is a really popular vegetarian oasis which also caters for gluten intolerance, dairy free and low cholesterol diets. It's so good, it became one of the first food venues to receive the Heart of Mersey award. Now, 14 years on, it still retains its unique charming atmosphere.

If you want a great lunch be sure to visit or call ahead on 0151 707 8592.

## Claire Kenny

Every now and then you meet someone who really lives their job and makes an immediate first impression – Claire (who will proudly tell you she is a 1st Assistant at our local McDonald's) loves her job and was a great help when we were thinking about our cafés and how our customer service should work. McDonald's should be proud. Thanks Claire.